CW00504637

CASTLES IN THE SEA
all about icebergs

Lawrence Jackson

Illustrations by Diana Dabinett

© 2000, Laura Jackson

Le Conseil des Arts | The Canada Council
du Canada | for the Arts

We acknowledge the support of The Canada Council for the Arts for our publishing program.

We acknowledge the financial support of the Government of Canada through the Book Publishing Industry Development Program (BPIDP) for our publishing activities.

All rights reserved. No part of this work covered by the copyrights hereon may be reproduced or used in any form or by any means—graphic, electronic or mechanical—without the prior written permission of the publisher. Any requests for photocopying, recording, taping or information storage and retrieval systems of any part of this book shall be directed in writing to the Canadian Reprography Collective, One Yonge Street, Suite 1900, Toronto, Ontario M5E 1E5.

Illustrations © 2000, Diana Dabinett

∞ Printed on acid-free paper

Published by
TUCKAMORE BOOKS
an imprint of CREATIVE BOOK PUBLISHING
a Transcontinental associated company
P.O. Box 8660, St. John's, NL A1B 3T7

First Edition April 2000
Second Printing September 2004
Third Printing June 2006

Printed in Canada by:
TRANSCONTINENAL

Canadian Cataloguing in Publication Data

Jackson, Lawrence, 1942-1998
    Castles in the sea
    ISBN 1-894294-17-3 (pbk) — ISBN 1-894294-23-8 (bound)

1. Icebergs — Juvenile literature. I. Dabinett, Diana, 1943-
II. Title.

GB2403.8.J33 2000   j551.34'2   C00-950101-0

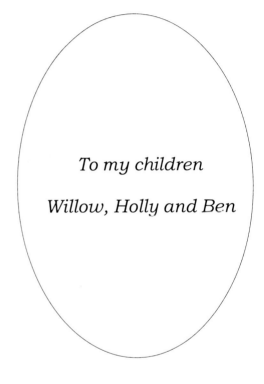

To my children

Willow, Holly and Ben

Acknowledgements

Additional text and editing by
Laura Jackson and
Janet McNaughton

Photography of silks by Ned Pratt

Design by Diana Dabinett

Valuable ideas and help given by
Anne Hart
Nora Flynn
Penelope Dexter
Willow Jackson

Dr. Stephen Bruneau
Dr. Don Murphy from the
International Ice Patrol

Denny Christian,
Dr. Richard McKenna
and Karen Muggeridge,
all from C-CORE

Dr. Greg Crocker of
Ballicater Consulting Ltd.

Joan Clark
Jack Clark

And thanks also to
Don Morgan, for his faith in
this project
Hilary Walsh, for listening

*A portion of the royalties from this book
will be donated to the
Lawrence Jackson Writers Award.*

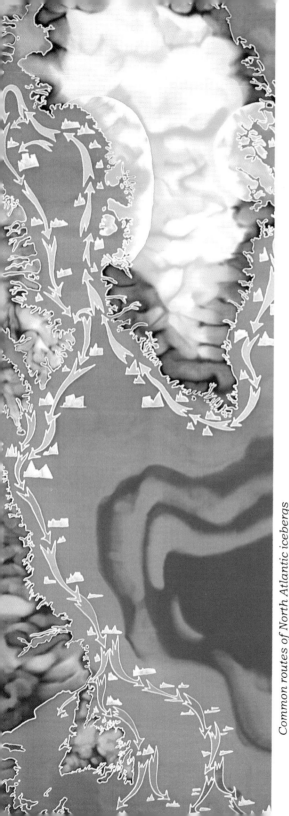

Common routes of North Atlantic icebergs

Ice Vocabulary—Newfoundland and Labrador

Newfoundlanders have developed a rich vocabulary to describe ice conditions. Often nouns are used as verbs, as in "ballicattering," or adjectives, as in "quarried." The following examples were selected from the Dictionary of Newfoundland English, Second Ed., 1998.

bergy bits = very small icebergs, but bigger than growlers

ballicatter = ice formed by the action of waves along the shoreline, making a fringe or band on the landward side; a narrow band of ice formed in winter in the salt water along the foreshore or landwash. There are more than 30 versions of this word, such as belly-carders, ballacattle, belliclumper and cattibatter.

clumper/clamper/clumber/clumpet/clampet = piece of drift ice; large chunk of ice floating in a bay or harbour

glim/ice-blink = glow or brightness seen over a distant ice field; shimmer over ice; dazzle of the ice at sea

growlers = iceberg pieces less than five meters at the waterline, or about the size of a grand piano, so named because of the sound they make when tossing in sea swells/large swells; "a berg which trembles on the verge of toppling over," wrote a traveller in 1906

ice-pan = loose piece of floating ice with a flat surface; piece of flat ice, roughly circular

ice-rind = thin layer of ice on water recently frozen or "caught" over; a thin, elastic crust of ice, formed by the freezing of slush or sludge on a quiet sea surface; thickness less than 2 inches, easily broken by wind or swell, and makes a tinkling noise when passed through by a ship

jam or jamb = a field of salt-water floe-ice so tightly packed that a ship can't get through it

local ice = ice formed in bays and harbours, or in the "leads" (channels of open water) between masses of drift ice from arctic or Labrador waters

quarry or quor = water that, by freezing, chokes or blocks up a channel; an area blocked with slush and then frozen

raft/rafter/rifter = type of pressure-ice/screw-ice formed by one floe overriding another; a sheet of ice forced up on shore; large sheet of ice tilted or forced up by pressure of the sea

rafting = the forcing of sheets of ice into tumbled masses; ice being forced to buckle and override other ice, sometimes in layers to a height of 30 or 40 feet

sish/swish/brash ice = fine, granulated ice floating on the surface of the sea; ice scum

sishy/shishy/shee-shee = made up of loose fragments of floating ice

slob/slub/slobice/sludge = heavy, slushy, densely packed mass of ice fragments, snow and freezing water, especially on the surface of the sea

young ice = salt-water ice from 5-15.2 cm (2-6") thick, newly-formed in the bays and harbours; primary stage of formation of level shore ice, generally in transition stage of development from ice-rind or pancake ice to winter-ice; still won't hold a person's weight

Far away, in a land too cold for forests, snow keeps falling every year.

Not much, because this is a land where the air is almost too cold, even for snow.

But some snow falls every year. And summer in this land is so brief and chilly that hardly any snow melts, even in August.

This place is called Greenland, where most of the land is not green. Greenland is nearly all rock. The name is just a trick.

Year after year the snow keeps piling up until it covers the mountains and fills the valleys, even in summer. The weight of all that snow, piling deeper and deeper, squeezes the part at the bottom until it turns into ice.

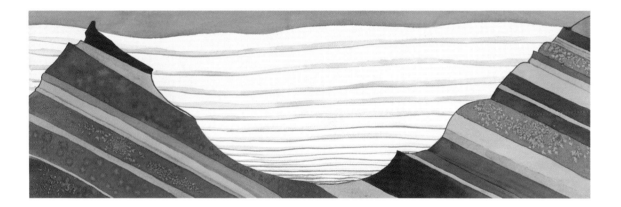

The Greenland Ice Sheet

Some icebergs come from Canada's arctic islands, but most icebergs in the North Atlantic are from the continental ice sheet of Greenland. This huge expanse of ice covers 1.7 million square kilometres (km) and is 3 km thick. Parts of this ice cap are 100,000 years old.

About 10 of the roughly 100 glaciers in West Greenland produce most of the icebergs. Mountains at the edges of the ice sheet force the glaciers through deep valleys before they reach the sea.

Year after year, for thousands of years, the snow keeps on falling, and the ice gets thicker and thicker until it buries nearly all the land.

How Glaciers Form

Glaciers are rivers of ice. They form when the weather is too cold for snow to melt. Alpine glaciers form on mountains while continental glaciers form on larger land masses.

Over hundreds of years, layers of snow build up, and the lower layers gradually become ice. When 60 to 70 metres collect, the pressure of the ice is so great that the bottom layer begins to "creep" or flow like a thick liquid, and a glacier is formed.

Between 10,000 and 40,000 icebergs are calved each year in Greenland. About 1,000 of those will reach as far south as Cape Bonavista in Newfoundland.

Finally, part of the ice gets so thick and heavy that it begins to slide down the mountain valleys across the bedrock body of Greenland.

It's as if the ice remembers it used to be water, and water's job is to find the sea.

It has become a glacier — a very slow river of ice, flowing down the valleys, looking for the sea.

How Fast Glaciers Move

Continental glaciers move more slowly than alpine glaciers. Greenland glaciers can be very slow, but some are among the fastest continental glaciers in the world, moving as much as 7 to 11 km per year.

In the narrow, steep-sided fjords at Jakobshavn and Quarayaq, glaciers advance 20 to 30 metres a day, as fast as the fastest alpine glacier. Still, most are much slower.

Because they move so slowly and travel so far, ice in the Greenland glaciers is frozen for thousands of years before it reaches the sea.

A glacier slides very slowly. In a whole year, one might move only the length of your arm, while another might cover the same distance in a day.

A glacier picks up loose rocks underneath as it moves, and uses them like sandpaper, scraping and smoothing the bedrock underneath. The ice slides out through the mountain valleys, grinding the rocks down and rounding them off, rubbing them smooth as apples.

Eventually, the smooth, solid body of Greenland is gone.

The glacier has reached the North Atlantic Ocean.

Photo courtesy of US Coast Guard

Most glaciers calve on the west coast of Greenland, but this shows icebergs emerging from a glacier on the east coast of Baffin Island in Canada's Arctic.

Canada's Ice Island

Ice islands are different from regular icebergs since they break off from ice shelves instead of glaciers, and contain some salt water. They are flat, and can be up to 40 km in diameter. All Northern Hemisphere ice islands calve from Ellesmere Island in Canada's Arctic.

Canadian scientists used one ice island near the North Pole from 1984 to 1991 as a research base for Arctic study. Its surface was 8 by 4 km, it was as deep as a 14-storey building, and it weighed about a billion tonnes.

Special equipment measured the ocean currents, and how much heat from the earth's crust was reaching the seabed mud. Scientists tracked air pollution as it circled the globe and studied tiny sea animals called plankton.

Photo by Lawrence Jackson

It took scientists on Canada's Ice Island 33 hours to drill a hole through its ice.

Things are suddenly very different.

Rock is steady, but water jiggles in the wind. Swelling with the tides, heaving and yearning this way and that, the ocean reaches for the moon but keeps slipping back.

Rocked with all this movement, the ice fractures and cracks.

Roaring like thunder, huge pieces break off to go where the ocean takes them. That's how icebergs are born.

When part of a glacier falls into the sea to become an iceberg, people call it "calving." Cows and whales give birth to calves, but glaciers calve icebergs.

Icebergs are pure as fresh snow and shiny as diamonds. They can be as small as a tree-house or as big as a skyscraper, towering above the sea. They are the grandest things many people ever see.

Photo by Janice L. Smith

Icebergs tower beyond the small Newfoundland community of Herring Neck, New World Island, Notre Dame Bay, near Twillingate.

Icebergs float in the very cold ocean, far in the north, with whales and seals diving and splashing around them, and seabirds stopping to rest on their icy shoulders.

They don't melt much, because the air and water are so cold. But they do melt a little, especially where waves come splashing against them. After awhile, they begin to take on wonderful shapes. Sometimes they look like huge white castles, with blue lights gleaming inside.

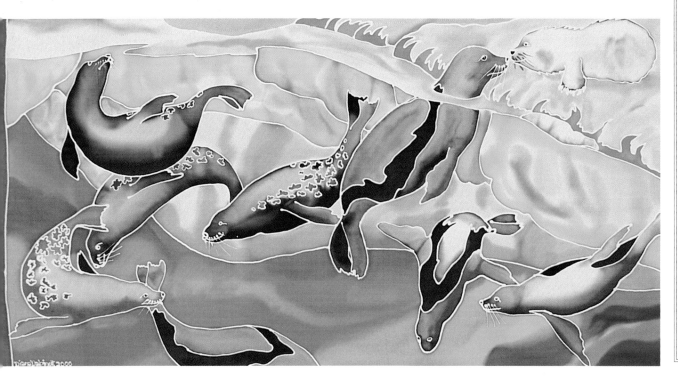

Most Common Iceberg Shapes

tabular	long and horizontal or flat-topped, like a table
blocky	chunky; steep-sided with a flat top
wedge	thicker along one side than the other; wedge-shaped
dome	large, smooth and rounded
pinnacled	having spires or pyramid shape; appearance of sharp mountain peaks
drydock	eroded so that a large U-shaped hollow is formed between columns on each side

An iceberg sinks a long, long way into the sea.
No matter how big it looks, you see just a little part of it;
the rest is out of sight under the surface of the ocean.
And since most of an iceberg is underwater,
it goes where the water says it must,
following currents that move through the seas
like powerful saltwater rivers.

Water is always going somewhere.
Some of the water up north, where icebergs are born,
joins the Greenland Current,
and eventually sweeps southward
into the Labrador Current,
along the coast of Labrador
to Newfoundland,
bringing icebergs with it.

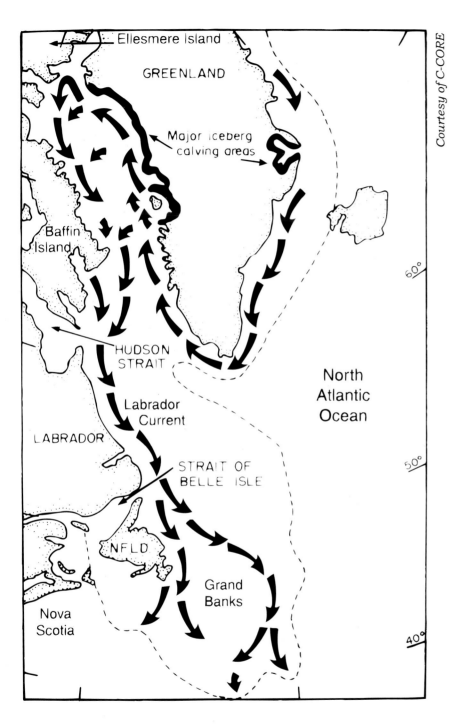

Courtesy of C-CORE

In a journey that can take two to three years, these currents bring thousands of icebergs south, so many that people call this stretch of ocean "Iceberg Alley."

Map of the routes taken by most North Atlantic icebergs.

C-CORE:

Studying Icebergs

The C-CORE research centre is part of Memorial University of Newfoundland in St. John's.

To companies searching for offshore oil and gas, the icebergs off Newfoundland create problems not found anywhere else in the world. C-CORE looks for solutions to these special problems —by locating icebergs with satellite radar imagery, measuring the damage they might do, and even finding ways to tow them out of the path of ships and drill rigs.

Iceberg water is now being sold as bottled water. C-CORE helps companies harvest icebergs safely.

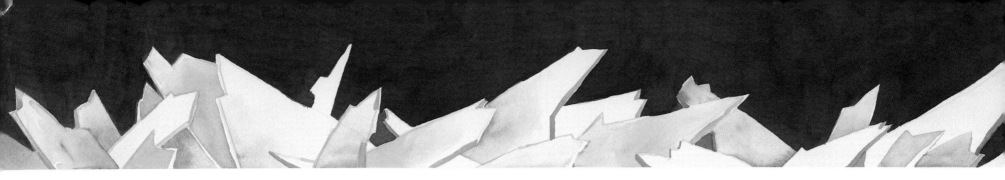

There's another kind of ice at sea, salty "pack ice" that forms each year on the surface, when it's very cold in the far north. It's a crust, like ice on a pond, and in the north it can be almost as flat as a pond.

But as it drifts farther south, swept along with the Labrador Current, this pack ice starts to melt. Waves begin to break it up, bashing pieces together and piling them up on top of each other. These pieces freeze together, break up again, then smash against each other as waves toss them around. After awhile, pack ice can look like a sea of broken dishes.

This is the kind of ice wind really likes, because it's all jumbled and complicated. When pack ice is smooth, like ice on a lake, the wind just skates across it. But ice with broken surfaces gives wind something to push and play with.

Underneath, this pack ice is just as messy, with lots of broken pieces sticking down. These jagged pieces grab the water like claws and fingers. When wind gets pack ice moving, the ice tugs at the water beneath.

Some icebergs have been clocked at nearly 4 kilometres per hour (kph), but most drift at an average speed of about 1 kph.

In 1882, the largest iceberg ever recorded in the Northern Hemisphere was found. It weighed over 9 billion tonnes and was 13 km long — enough water to give everyone in the world a litre a day for over 4 years! Icebergs from Antarctica can be even larger – one was 150 km long.

When birds suddenly take flight from an iceberg, it may mean the iceberg is about to roll. Scientists believe that birds' keen sense of balance may help them detect small movements long before people could.

Now, something neat happens. Remember the iceberg, drifting along in the ocean? Floating so deep in the water, an iceberg usually goes where the currents take it. The wind can't normally move something as huge as an iceberg. It just slides off its smooth and slippery shoulders.

But when wind catches the pack ice and pack ice catches the water, small icebergs in the way can be dragged along as well. Huge icebergs driven by deep sea currents can plow through pack ice like an icebreaker, but smaller icebergs can suddenly find themselves travelling with the wind.

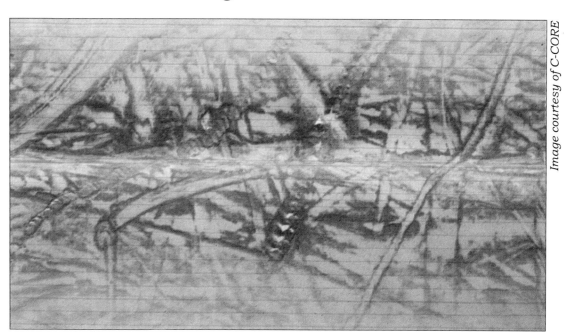

Image courtesy of C-CORE

Sonar image of iceberg "scour" marks on the Grand Banks, some perhaps as old as 12,000 years. "Relic scours" are those more than 10,000 years old, whereas "recent" ones are less than 10,000.

These gouges scraped into the seabed by giant icebergs can be many kilometres long.

Sometimes the wind blows onshore, bringing pack ice and icebergs with it. Some icebergs are so big they dig into the sea-bottom and "ground" themselves near shore. Then people get to admire them for a long time, and watch them change shape as they slowly melt.

All one summer, people in a Newfoundland village called Outer Cove could look out their kitchen windows and see seven giant icebergs, like seven gleaming castles, stuck on a shoal offshore.

Imagine a huge and ancient fortress of ice above the sea. Now picture another part underneath, seven times bigger, lurking below the surface of the water.

Imagine how dangerous icebergs are for ships in the North Atlantic.

The famous passenger liner, *Titanic*, steamed into an iceberg one April night in 1912, not far from Newfoundland.

But the *Titanic* is only the best known of many ships that have sunk to the bottom of the sea after colliding with icebergs.

Painting by Laurie Lacey

While painting this impression of the Titanic disaster, the artist studied a 1912 photograph of the iceberg which the famous ship may have hit.

Photo courtesy of US Coast Guard

International Ice Patrol

After the *Titanic* sank in 1912, 13 countries formed the International Ice Patrol to reduce the danger of ice to ships in the North Atlantic. Every spring from February on, US Coast Guard aircraft track icebergs. Ships also report iceberg sightings to the Canadian Ice Service (CIS).

Tracking icebergs has changed since 1912. Radar now lets planes "see" icebergs through the thickest fog. The CIS uses images beamed down from the RADARSAT satellite, with information about ocean currents and winds, to predict where icebergs will travel.

A daily "Ice Bulletin," broadcast on radio and the World Wide Web, warns ships of dangers.

As the air and water get warmer, icebergs begin to melt, and as they do they gradually change their shape. After awhile they may become top-heavy and suddenly roll over. You'd better not be close when they do. Imagine a castle turning a somersault!

Small boats try to keep a safe distance from icebergs, because when one rolls over it makes huge waves. Pieces break off with explosions like cannons or gunshots, as millions of tiny air bubbles trapped under great pressure inside the ice suddenly burst free.

Death of an Iceberg

Icebergs can break into many pieces before melting away completely. Waves splashing at the waterline create a notch which causes the ice above and below to fracture more quickly. Caves, tunnels and arches can also form.

Water temperature makes a big difference in the time it takes an iceberg to melt. In water at 0 degrees Celsius (the normal freezing point of fresh water), a large iceberg may take 3 months or more to melt. But in 10-degree water, the same iceberg could disappear in just 1 to 2 weeks.

If pack ice or icebergs survive to travel past Newfoundland, they quickly melt in the warmer water. Few icebergs go farther south but, even so, an iceberg may travel 4,000 km before it dies.

Photo courtesy of C-CORE

A small boat is dwarfed by this iceberg that weighs an estimated 50,000 tonnes. Bubble-free ice has a blue tint.

If you remember that all this began with snowflakes — billions and billions of them falling on Greenland — you can guess where those little bubbles came from. Any pile of newly-fallen snow is mostly air. When you make a snowball, you squeeze most of the air out, but a little bit always remains.

It's the same with the snow that's been falling on Greenland for thousands of years. When all that snow got too heavy, the bottom turned into ice, but some air stayed trapped deep inside. As more and more ice piled up, the weight put tremendous pressure on those little bubbles, squeezing them so small they seemed to disappear.

Now, they're like millions of invisible balloons, ready to burst.

Imagine you've just put a piece of iceberg in your apple juice. Hold your breath and listen to the chorus of tiny explosions that erupts inside your glass. Hold your nose over the glass and smell the cleanest air in the world, air just freed from bubbles that may be 40,000 years old.

There were no streets or cities when that air was trapped. The last creature to breathe that air before you might have been a woolly mammoth or a sabre-tooth tiger, animals that don't exist today.

And when you sip your apple juice as it melts the ice, you'll be drinking the purest water on earth, water that may have evaporated from a tropical sea all those thousands of years ago, and drifted north on high winds over the earth.

This is water that fell as lovely, delicate snowflakes on the bedrock of Greenland, back when people wore skins and lived in caves.

This is water that almost forgot what it was like to be water, because it was ice for so long.

Take a tiny piece of this ice, warm it in your hand, and help it start all over again.